ART OF RUNNING

Photo Anthology / Peter Slater

"The miracle isn't that I finished. The miracle is that I had the courage to start."
John Bingham

"Run when you can, walk if you have to, crawl if you must; just never give up."
Dean Karnazes

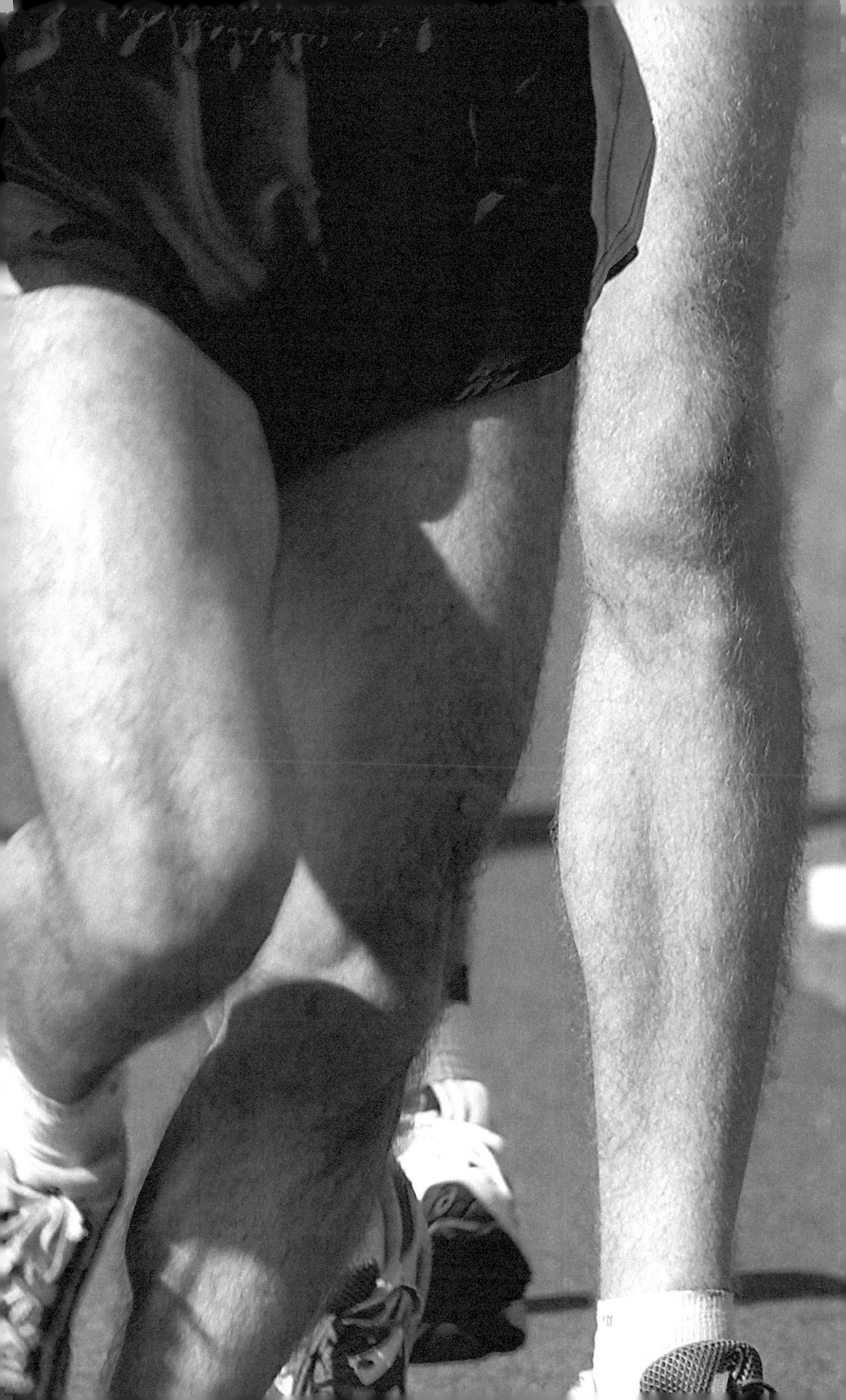

"I don't run to add days to my life, I run to add life to my days."
Ronald Rook

"The point is whether or not I improved over yesterday. In long-distance running the only opponent you have to beat is yourself, the way you used to be."
Haruki Murakami

"Every morning in Africa, a gazelle wakes up, it knows it must outrun the fastest lion or it will be killed. Every morning in Africa, a lion wakes up. It knows it must run faster than the slowest gazelle, or it will starve. It doesn't matter whether you're the lion or a gazelle – when the sun comes up, you'd better be running."
Christopher McDougall

"Running! If there's any activity happier, more exhilarating, more nourishing to the imagination, I can't think of what it might be. In running the mind flees with the body, the mysterious efflorescence of language seems to pulse in the brain, in rhythm with our feet and the swinging of our arms."
Joyce Carol Oates

"Pain is temporary. Quitting lasts forever."
Lance Armstrong

"Your body will argue that there is no justifiable reason to continue. Your only recourse is to call on your spirit, which fortunately functions independently of logic."Tim Noakes

"You can keep going and your legs might hurt for a week or you can quit and your mind will hurt for a lifetime.

Mark Allen

"If you are losing faith in human nature, go out and watch a marathon."
Kathrine Switzer

"There is nothing so momentary as a sporting achievement, and nothing so lasting as the memory of it."
Greg Dening

"You need to save some mental, physical, and emotional resources for enhancing your product after you ship. A revolution is a triathlon, not a hundred-yard dash-it requires long distance stamina and multiple skills such as creating, churning, and evangelizing.
Guy Kawasaki

"Triathlon – It's not about finding your limits. It's about finding out what lies just beyond them.

unknown

"It's rude to count people as you pass them. Out loud

unknown

"As your training moves from base training to more intense work, to tapering, your nutrition needs to change.
Charlotte Campbell

"Almost drowned, crashed the bike, puked on the run. When's the next Tri?

unknown

www.ingramcontent.com/pod-product-compliance
Lightning Source LLC
Chambersburg PA
CBHW021251280526
45784CB00005B/2327